Beverly Barrett Flintom
Founder of Your Card Is Your Destiny
yourcardisyourdestiny.com

DEDICATION

This book is dedicated to my mother and my son. I always felt that my mother was a true Queen and it turns out she is; A Queen of Clubs ♣ the most intuitive card in the deck, a Three of Diamonds ♦ and Jack of Hearts ♥. She can read people quicker than anyone I know. She is also the most compassionate, kind and loving person and I am truly blessed to have her in my life.

To my son, Denver. When I prayed to God to bring me a righteous man, he did. He answered my prayers by bringing me Denver, a Two of Spades ♠; The Friendship Card and a Six of Spades ♠ card of fate, no joke. So remember when you pray be specific! He has taught me so much and because of him, I was able to study and befriend dozens of young adults who I hope will take this knowledge and share it with the world. Also, to all my friends who believed in me and allowed me to put this system to the test for its undeniable accuracy! Special thanks to my dear friend Tracy Boehmer Jack of Diamonds ♦ and Two of Spades ♠ for helping me complete and publish this handbook. I Love You All!

Finally, my late Father Four of Diamonds ♦ and Six of Spades ♠, Sister and Brother (twins) Four of Spades ♠ and Ace of Diamonds ♦ who have crossed to the other side and come to me in my dreams to let me know that they are only a thought away. Until we meet again.

May you find the acceptance of who you are and the validation of why you have always felt a certain way. May this Little Book of Secrets help you on your Journey.

Warmly,

One of many JOKERS ♥♣♦♠
Beverly Barrett Flintom

Table of Contents

INTRODUCTION

Twelve years ago, I came across a book that changed my life. It was called "Love Cards, by Robert Camp. For the first time I finally saw in writing who I was. The accuracy of myself, my family and my friends were described to a tee. I went on to buy another one of his books called, "Cards of Destiny." I began to study these books daily and began doing readings on my family and friends. A few years went by and I knew that my next mission in life was to share this information with the world. Since then I have also studied with Sharon Jeffers author of "Love & Destiny" and added another book to study called "Face Value" by Gina E. Jones. In 2011 I founded Your Card Is Your Destiny and took a leap of faith and decided that sharing this knowledge with the world was my destiny.

A few years ago I had the honor of building a friendship with Gina E. Jones and like me, she believed this card reading system should be available for the world to know. Last year she created the ***International Association of Cardology (IAC)*** and asked me along with 11 other experts around the world to become founding members. I was honored. This card reading system has been kept secret for thousands of years but is now available for those who seek the truth of who they really are. There are many names for this system but as founding members we are unifying and calling this system ***Cardology***, study of the ancient metaphysical science of playing cards.

Each day of the year, your birthday is ruled by one of the 53 cards in our playing deck of cards including the JOKER. It is ancient wisdom that has been protected for thousands of years. Each card has certain characteristics that establish your personality and the way you see the world, the way you interact with others and also determines the path you are intended to live. With each card we have a choice to come from the high side of the card or the low side of the card and we also have a choice on whether or not we will accept the card we are dealt or not. The choice is ours.

This system can determine and predict what will happen each year of your life. Every birthday, you receive a new forecast for the year. However, your birth cards and personality cards remain the same your entire life.

This book only gives brief definitions of your cards. If you would like to understand more than is described, at the back of this book is a list of authors that I would recommend.

Destiny Cards are considered Scientific & Mathematic

The deck of playing cards and our calendar coincide. This information is ancient and can be proven scientifically and mathematically.

Here is the breakdown:

52 cards/52 weeks in a year
Numerology breaks down the numbers: 5 + 2 = 7   Seven days in a week & 7 visible Planets

4 Suits==4 Seasons

When we add a numeric number to the cards it is as follows:
Ace/1
2/2
3/3
4/4
5/5
6/6
7/7
8/8
9/9
10/10
Jack/11
Queen/12
King/13

When we add up all the numbers of the entire deck we come to 364. The JOKER value is 1 and ¼ the number comes to 365, the number of days in our calendar year.

At the back of this book you will find birthday charts that will tell you your birth card. All of the birthdays have 2 cards, some have 3 and there are 2 birthdays that have 4 cards.

The first card is your Birth card that explains the traits you exhibit in your life. The second card is called your Personality card. The best way to understand the difference is that the Birth card is how you feel and the Personality card is usually how you show yourself to the world. From my experience I have noticed that most people show their 2nd card more so than the Birth card. For those that have 3 and 4 cards, notice the &/or they can exhibit any and all of the personalities of those cards.

SUITS

HEART
Rule Emotion

The Enlightened Heart knows compassion

You know that saying "they wear their heart on their sleeve?" Well, these people's personalities are just like the quote. They literally do! However, they may not always show that side of themselves. They are understanding, compassionate and kind. They are also very sensitive, emotional and are very youthful. They are the adults that never really grow up! They feel everything.

High Side
Fun, loving and great to have around to literally console the broken-hearted.

Low Side
Tearful, emotional, sulky and can act like a child when upset.

They are the FEELER'S in the Group.

CLUB
Rule the Mind

The Enlightened Club has understanding

You know your friends that watch TV to go to sleep at night or are constantly on their phones? They are probably a Club Card! The reason for this is that they can never get their mind to rest! They are the thinkers of the group. They analyze things to death; literally they also love to talk whether on the phone, on text or in person. When you get a text from them it will never be a sentence it will be a paragraph! Their minds need constant stimulation.

High Side
They will help you come up with a solution or two. They are very good at organization and can solve any puzzle in your life.

Low Side
Worry and stress and their words can be like weapons.

They are the THINKERS and ANALYZERS in the Group.

DIAMOND
Rule the material world

The Enlightened Diamond moves with Integrity

You know the people that "look like a million bucks?" Most likely they are a diamond card. They are always the best dressed in a crowd of people and like to sparkle just like a diamond. Money and or the Value of something are prominent on their minds.

High Side
Fun loving. Free spirited. Always brighten things up when they are around.

Low Side
They run when things get difficult. Let them go and they will always return.

They are mostly concerned with the VALUE of things.

SPADE

Rule the Spiritual World

The Enlightened Spade is Wise

You know those people that act first and then ask questions later? They are probably a Spade card. They are the "doers" of the suits. They are also the oldest souls in the deck. They also come to this life with the most spiritual wisdom. If you want something done, ask a Spade.

High Side
Can accomplish anything they put their mind to.

Low Side
Stubborn won't bend or move.

They are the DOERS in the group.

SYMBOLS or Simply Defined

Card		Symbol
Ace	A	Initiators
Two	2	Partnerships
Three	3	Creativity
Four	4	Security
Five	5	Adventure
Six	6	Balance
Seven	7	Spiritual
Eight	8	Power
Nine	9	Universal
Ten	10	Independent
Jack	J	Clever
Queen	Q	Mothers
Kings	K	Masters

CARDS

ACE

Initiators, Beginners & Desire

ACE of Heart ♥

First card in the deck. Independent, ambitious, impulsive and flirtatious. Always desire to create something new. Hearts rule relationships.

ACE of Clubs ♣

Seeker of knowledge. Quick humor. Always in search of the perfect mate. Always asking why?

ACE of Diamonds ♦

Driven. Passionate. Money. Worth. Value. Some cannot decide if they want money or love in their life.

ACE of Spades ♠

Workaholics. Secretive. Most ambitious and materialistic in the deck. Conflict between materialistic and spiritual heritage. You will always see this card on the cover of most decks of cards because in this card lies the secrets and the wisdom in our deck of cards.

Aces are ambitious and are always in search of self. All ACES struggle with selfishness versus the needs for others. They are inventors and initiators. Their ideas are futuristic.

TWO

Partnerships & Union

2 of Hearts ♥

Prefers having a partner in Love. As with all two's they would rather have any partner than none at all.

2 of Clubs ♣

Likes to communicate with a partner to share ideas. They can be witty and charming. When fearful they will become irritable and argumentative.

2 of Diamonds ♦

Prefers having a partner in business. They are the "wheeler dealers" of the group.

2 of Spades ♠

Likes to have a partner in work. Friends are very important to them and they usually have dozens of friends. Has a tendency to be stubborn.

All 2's experience greater success when in a partnership. They are the best debaters in the deck of cards. The challenge for them is to be positive versus negative and to learn how to cooperate in a partnership. Most 2's do not like to ever be alone.

THREE

Creativity & Indecision

3 of Hearts ♥

Emotionally creative and likes variety in Love. Always feels indecision when it comes to love.

3 of Clubs ♣

Mentally creative and needs variety in work and in love. One of the most creative in the deck. Can be successful in any creative field they choose.

3 of Diamonds ♦

Creative in finances and business. If you need an idea they are sure to have a drawer full of ideas. The most difficult life path in the deck mostly with personal relationships.

3 of Spades ♠

Creative with work projects and work. Should always do something creative in their professional life.

All 3's must be doing something creative in their life to avoid stress and worry. Most 3's will always feel that they are split in two different directions.

FOUR

Stability & Protection

4 of Hearts ♥

Desires stability in love and family. Usually puts the needs of others before themselves.

4 of Clubs ♣

Desires stability and mental satisfaction. Likes to exchange ideas with others and needs to have mental stimulation to be happy. Also likes a lot of attention.

4 of Diamonds ♦

Desires stability in finances. Must work hard for their money to reap rewards.

4 of Spades ♠

Desires stability in work. Will only feel satisfied if their work life is gratifying. Most stable card in the deck.

All 4's crave security and stability in their suit or they become anxious and difficult. 4's have one of the most fortunate and blessed life paths.

FIVE

Adventurous & Restless

5 of Hearts ♥

Enjoys a lot of adventures with the heart. Changes mind a lot concerning love. Can become emotionally restless.

5 of Clubs ♣

Mentally restless. Dislikes routine and usually constantly on the go. Happy when discovering new things and new places.

5 of Diamonds ♦

Always moving and dislikes anything that limits their freedom. Best salesperson in the deck. Money comes in and out of their life.

5 of Spades ♠

Likes changes in work and travel. Moves to new homes frequently. Always striving for the truth and need to develop inner self.

5's are the most adventurous and are the most fun to be around. All 5's are restless and non-committal. Always moving and changing is a constant theme in a 5's life.

SIX

Balance & Karma

6 of Hearts ♥

Likes to keep the peace. Must learn responsibility in love relationships. Lots of lessons in one's lifetime concerning relationships.

6 of Clubs ♣

Lessons come in the mental field for these folks. Instant Karma for things said. Most do not realize their psychic ability.

6 of Diamonds ♦

Have many lessons with money. They either pay their bills in advance or are always worrying about money or spend it as fast as they get it.

6 of Spades ♠

Fated events occur frequently. Karma acts quickly and swiftly with this card. Usually an action oriented event.

Most Karmic card in the deck. All 6's have instant karma related to their suit. They are either not responsible or overly responsible. Most are very psychic.

SEVEN

Spiritual & Guided

7 of Hearts ♥

Seeks Spiritual Love. Concerned with personal relationships and love. Makes a lot of sacrifices for family.

7 of Clubs ♣

Seeks Knowledge and understanding. Analytical and observant. Must always trust information received from the spiritual realm or will get stuck in negativity.

7 of Diamonds ♦

Some are destined to become millionaires as long as they do not let money rule their life. Everything for them is based on faith from God or a Higher being. If they trust in themselves and what they know to be true, everything turns out well.

7 of Spades ♠

The card of Faith and the most mystical in the deck. They are here to learn to trust their innate intuition and to trust the information they receive.

All 7's need to trust their Spiritual self for things to go smoothly. If not, challenges & jealousy arise frequently. Sevens can also become negative when they are fearful.

EIGHT

Power & Abundance

8 of Hearts ♥

Emotional power and abundance. Charm & magnetism. They are the playboy/playgirl of the deck.

8 of Clubs ♣

Power in communications and thought. Mentally powerful. One of the three fixed cards in the deck, meaning they will not change their mind unless it serves them in some way.

8 of Diamonds ♦

Power and abundance in money. Can make a lot of money but likes to spend it as fast as they earn the money.

8 of Spades ♠

Power and abundance in work. Usually has much success in the area of work.

8's are the power cards and most have successful life paths. All 8's must not misuse their power. If they do they can become abusive and overly stubborn.

NINE

Universal & Completion

9 of Hearts ♥

Universal. Giver of love. Many beginnings and endings in personal relationships.

9 of Clubs ♣

Universal. Giver of Knowledge. Here to spread knowledge in a big way. They all have a message to spread to the world.

9 of Diamonds ♦

Universal. Giver of money. Usually has times of money losses throughout their life. If they understand that letting go of the money it will surely come back to them.

9 of Spades ♠

Universal Givers in work. Most 9 of spades have a lot of job beginnings and endings. Can also struggle with health issues as well.

The challenge for all 9's is letting go of people, things, work and health. For a 9, it feels as though they have a graduation year every year of their life. They must accept endings in which can create new beginnings for them. For without endings, we would never have beginnings. 9's are all about letting go.

TEN

Success with groups

10 of Hearts ♥

Success with groups of people. Many entertainers are this card and enjoy the stage and the lime light.

10 of Clubs ♣

The teacher and healer. Extremely intelligent. Very independent in nature.

10 of Diamonds ♦

The Blessing Card. Usually good at managing business and usually receive money from inheritance or other unexpected ways.

10 of Spades ♠

Success with work in groups. Very effective as a manager of business and works very hard. Usually to the point that their personal life is sacrificed.

All 10's do things in a big way. They are independent and need freedom in relationships to be happy. They can be egotistical.

JACK

Clever & Witty

Jack of Hearts ♥

1 of the 3 Fixed Cards in the deck meaning they are not budging until compelled to do so. They usually make a lot of sacrifices for their family. Sometimes act like a martyr.

Jack of Clubs ♣

Clever. Witty. Creativity meets intelligence. Crafty & Cunning. Immature at times. Can be dishonest.

Jack of Diamonds ♦

The Salesmen Card. Clever with money related projects. Very independent. Extremely creative.

Jack of Spades ♠

The Actor Card. Highly intelligent and creative. Can accomplish anything they choose to do.

All JACKS are clever and are considered the princess in the deck. If they operate out of the low side of the card they can be dishonest and crafty.

QUEEN

Mothering & Service Oriented

Queen of Hearts ♥

Loving Mother. Nurturing. Better parents than spouses. Can be lazy.

Queen of Clubs ♣

Mother of Intuition. Can read someone immediately if tapped into their innate intuition. Mother of Knowledge.

Queen of Diamonds ♦

Can be wonderful entrepreneurs. Usually has a harem of sorts. Money is very important.

Queen of Spades ♠

Mother of work. Work is extremely important for them and they have great organization ability.

All QUEENS are mothering in nature. May feel like smothering or overbearing at times.

KING

Masters & Leaders

King of Hearts ♥

Master of Love. Usually a better Father than spouse. Desires a large family or Kingdom in Love. Highest suit of Love.

King of Clubs ♣

Master of Knowledge. Born to lead. Can retain information with ease. Extremely intuitive.

King of Diamonds ♦

Master in Finance. Usually works with money in some way and many are self-employed. Best suited to own their own business and work for themselves.

King of Spades ♠

Highest card in mastery of work. One of the 3 fixed cards in the deck. Once they have made a decision about something no one can change their mind unless they choose to.

KINGS are the masters in their given suit. They are the highest cards in the deck. Most kings choose to run their own business as they are not found of being told what to do.

JOKER

Wild Card & Mysterious

The Alpha and the Omega, meaning they can be any suit and any card they choose at any given time. They are usually found to work in the arts and entertainment field. They are very mysterious and can even be a mystery unto themselves. The Joker bridges the Ace of Heart ♥ with the King of Spades ♠.

In old days, their birthday December 31st was a day of celebration for the new upcoming year. Therefore there is no yearly forecast for the JOKER.

The JOKER is all the cards and all the suits. Finally, now I know Who I Am but better yet, now you know Who You Are.

JOKER

BIRTH CHARTS

January

Day	Birth	Personality Card	Day	Birth Card	Personality Card
1	K ♠	5 ♣	16	J ♦	6 ♣
2	Q ♠	K ♣	17	10 ♦	5 ♥
3	J ♠	10 ♦	18	9 ♦	4 ♥
4	10 ♠	7 ♦	19	8 ♦	10 ♠
5	9 ♠	4 ♣	20	7 ♦	2 ♥
6	8 ♠	3 ♣	21	6 ♦	A ♥ or A ♦
7	7 ♠	4 ♦	22	5 ♦	K ♣
8	6 ♠	3 ♥	23	4 ♦	10 ♣
9	5 ♠	K ♥	24	3 ♦	9 ♣
10	4 ♠	A ♦	25	2 ♦	10 ♦
11	3 ♠	J ♣	26	A ♦	7 ♣
12	2 ♠	10 ♣	27	K ♣	6 ♣
13	A ♠	9 ♣	28	Q ♣	7 ♦
14	K ♦	8 ♣	29	J ♣	4 ♥
15	Q ♦	7 ♣	30	10 ♣	10 ♠
			31	9 ♣	4 ♣

February

Day	Birth	Personality Card	Day	Birth Card	Personality Card
1	J♠	8 ♠	16	9♦	4♦
2	10♠	5 ♠	17	8♦	5♣
3	9♠	2♦	18	7♦	K♥
4	8♠	3♠	19	6♦	A♦
5	7♠	2♠	20	5♦	K♣ or J♦
6	6♠	A♣	21	4♦	8♦
7	5♠	K♦	22	3♦	9♠
8	4♠	Q♦	23	2♦	8♠
9	3♠	9♦	24	A♦	5♦
10	2♠	8♦	25	K♣	6♠
11	A♠	9♠	26	Q♣	5♠
12	K♦	6♦	27	J♣	4♦
13	Q♦	5♦	28	10♣	5♣
14	J♦	6♠	29	9♣	2♦
15	10♦	3♣			

March

Day	Birth	Personality Card	Day	Birth Card	Personality Card
1	9♠	J♠	16	7♦	K♦
2	8♠	9♥	17	6♦	Q♦
3	7♠	8♥	18	5♦	J♦
4	6♠	Q♣	19	4♦	8♦
5	5♠	6♥	20	3♦	9♠ or 7♦
6	4♠	5♥	21	2♦	8♠ or 6♦
7	3♠	7♠	22	A♦	3♣
8	2♠	K♠	23	K♣	4♦
9	A♠	2♥	24	Q♣	3♦
10	K♦	4♠	25	J♣	2♣
11	Q♦	Q♠	26	10♣	3♥
12	J♦	Q♥	27	9♣	K♥
13	10♦	3♠	28	8♣	10♥
14	9♦	2♠	29	7♣	J♣
15	8♦	3♦	30	6♣	10♣
			31	5♣	7♥

April

Day	Birth	Personality Card	Day	Birth Card	Personality Card
1	7♠	J♦	16	5♦	9♦
2	6♠	8♦	17	4♦	6♣
3	5♠	9♠	18	3♦	7♦
4	4♠	8♠	19	2♦	6♦
5	3♠	5♦	20	A♦	3♣ or 5♥
6	2♠	6♠	21	K♣	4♦ or 4♥
7	A♠	5♠	22	Q♣	5♣
8	K♦	2♦	23	J♣	7♠
9	Q♦	3♠	24	10♣	K♠
10	J♦	2♠	25	9♣	2♥
11	10♦	A♦	26	8♣	4♠
12	9♦	K♣	27	7♣	Q♠
13	8♦	A♣	28	6♣	Q♥
14	7♦	9♣	29	5♣	A♠
15	6♦	10♦	30	4♣	J♠

May

Day	Birth	Personality Card	Day	Birth Card	Personality Card
1	5♠	9♣	16	3♦	7♥
2	4♠	10♦	17	2♦	8♣
3	3♠	7♣	18	A♦	5♥
4	2♠	6♣	19	K♣	4♥
5	A♠	7♦	20	Q♣	5♣ or 10♠
6	K♦	4♣	21	J♣	7♠ or 9♦
7	Q♦	3♣	22	10♣	K♠ or 8♦
8	J♦	4♦	23	9♣	9♠
9	10♦	A♥	24	8♣	6♦
10	9♦	2♣	25	7♣	5♦
11	8♦	3♥	26	6♣	6♠
12	7♦	J♥	27	5♣	3♦
13	6♦	10♥	28	4♣	2♦
14	5♦	J♣	29	3♣	3♠
15	4♦	8♥	30	2♣	K♣
			31	A♣	Q♣

June

Day	Birth	Personality Card	Day	Birth Card	Personality Card
1	3♠	9♥	16	A♦	Q♦
2	2♠	8♥	17	K♣	J♦
3	A♠	7♥	18	Q♣	10♠
4	K♦	6♥	19	J♣	9♦
5	Q♦	5♥	20	10♣	8♦
6	J♦	4♥	21	9♣	9♠
7	10♦	8♠	22	8♣	6♦ or J♠
8	9♦	7♠	23	7♣	9♥
9	8♦	K♠	24	6♣	8♥
10	7♦	5♠	25	5♣	10♠
11	6♦	4♠	26	4♣	6♥
12	5♦	Q♠	27	3♣	5♥
13	4♦	2♠	28	2♣	7♠
14	3♦	A♠	29	A♣	3♥
15	2♦	J♠	30	K♥	2♥

July

Day	Birth	Personality Card	Day	Birth Card	Personality Card
1	A♠	3♦	16	Q♣	A♣
2	K♦	K♥	17	J♣	Q♠
3	Q♦	A♦	18	10♣	Q♥
4	J♦	K♣	19	9♣	J♥
5	10♦	10♥	20	8♣	J♠
6	9♦	J♣	21	7♣	9♥
7	8♦	10♣	22	6♣	8♥
8	7♦	7♥	23	5♣	10♠ or 5♣
9	6♦	8♣	24	4♣	4♣
10	5♦	7♣	25	3♣	3♣
11	4♦	4♥	26	2♣	2♣
12	3♦	5♣	27	A♣	A♣
13	2♦	4♣	28	K♥	K♥
14	A♦	A♥	29	Q♥	Q♥
15	K♣	2♣	30	J♥	J♥
			31	10♥	10♥

August

Day	Birth	Personality Card	Day	Birth Card	Personality Card
1	Q♦	Q♦	16	10♣	10♣
2	J♦	J♦	17	9♣	9♣
3	10♦	10♦	18	8♣	8♣
4	9♦	9♦	19	7♣	7♣
5	8♦	8♦	20	6♣	6♣
6	7♦	7♦	21	5♣	5♣
7	6♦	6♦	22	4♣	4♣ or 2♦
8	5♦	5♦	23	3♣	3♣ or 3♠
9	4♦	4♦	24	2♣	K♣
10	3♦	3♦	25	A♣	Q♣
11	2♦	2♦	26	K♥	K♦
12	A♦	A♦	27	Q♥	10♣
13	K♣	K♣	28	J♥	9♣
14	Q♣	Q♣	29	10♥	10♦
15	J♣	J♣	30	9♥	7♣
			31	8♥	6♣

September

Day	Birth	Personality Card	Day	Birth Card	Personality Card
1	10♦	8♠	16	8♣	6♦
2	9♦	7♠	17	7♣	5♦
3	8♦	K♠	18	6♣	6♠
4	7♦	5♠	19	5♣	3♦
5	6♦	4♠	20	4♣	2♦
6	5♦	Q♠	21	3♣	3♠
7	4♦	2♠	22	2♣	K♣ or J♦
8	3♦	A♠	23	A♣	Q♣ or 10♠
9	2♦	J♠	24	K♥	6♥
10	A♦	Q♦	25	Q♥	8♦
11	K♣	J♦	26	J♥	9♠
12	Q♣	10♠	27	10♥	8♠
13	J♣	9♦	28	9♥	5♦
14	10♣	8♦	29	8♥	6♠
15	9♣	9♠	30	7♥	5♠

October

Day	Birth Card	Personality Card	Day	Birth Card	Personality Card
1	8♦	3♥	16	6♣	Q♥
2	7♦	J♥	17	5♣	A♠
3	6♦	10♥	18	4♣	J♠
4	5♦	J♣	19	3♣	9♥
5	4♦	8♥	20	2♣	J♦
6	3♦	7♥	21	A♣	10♠
7	2♦	8♣	22	K♥	6♥
8	A♦	5♥	23	Q♥	8♦ or K♠ & 5♣
9	K♣	4♥	24	J♥	9♥ or 2♥ & 2♦
10	Q♣	5♣	25	10♥	A♥ & 3♠
11	J♣	7♠	26	9♥	Q♠ & K♣
12	10♣	K♠	27	8♥	Q♥ & A♣
13	9♣	2♥	28	7♥	J♥ & K♦
14	8♣	4♠	29	6♥	J♠ & 10♦
15	7♣	Q♠	30	5♥	9♥ & 9♦
			31	4♥	8♥ & 8♦

November

Day	Birth Card	Personality Card		Day	Birth Card	Personality Card	
1	6♦	10♦	& 5♥	16	4♣	8♣	& 8♠
2	5♦	9♦	& 4♥	17	3♣	7♣	& 7♠
3	4♦	6♣	& K♠	18	2♣	4♥	& 6♠
4	3♦	7♦	& 2♥	19	A♣	5♣	& 5♠
5	2♦	6♦	& A♥	20	K♥	4♣	& 4♠
6	A♦	3♣	& Q♠	21	Q♥	K♠	& 5♣
7	K♣	4♦	& Q♥	22	J♥	2♥	& 2♦
8	Q♣	3♦	& J♥	23	10♥	A♦	
9	J♣	2♣	& 2♠	24	9♥	J♣	
10	10♣	3♥	& 3♦	25	8♥	10♣	
11	9♣	K♥	& J♠	26	7♥	9♣	
12	8♣	10♥	& Q♦	27	6♥	8♣	
13	7♣	J♣	& J♦	28	5♥	7♣	
14	6♣	10♣	& Q♣	29	4♥	6♣	
15	5♣	7♥	& 9♠	30	3♥	5♣	

December

Day	Birth Card	Personality Card	Day	Birth Card	Personality Card
1	4♦	6♠	16	2♣	4♦
2	3♦	5♠	17	A♣	3♦
3	2♦	4♠	18	K♥	2♦
4	A♦	3♠	19	Q♥	3♥
5	K♣	2♠	20	J♥	K♥
6	Q♣	A♠	21	10♥	A♦ or Q♦
7	J♣	K♣	22	9♥	J♣ or 9♦
8	10♣	A♣	23	8♥	8♦
9	9♣	K♦	24	7♥	9♠
10	8♣	10♦	25	6♥	6♦
11	7♣	9♦	26	5♥	5♦
12	6♣	8♦	27	4♥	6♠
13	5♣	7♦	28	3♥	3♦
14	4♣	6♦	29	2♥	2♦
15	3♣	5♦	30	A♥	3♠
			31	JOKER ♥♣♦♠	

REFERENCES

Love Cards: What Your Birthday Reveals About You and Your Personal Relationships by Robert Lee Camp
Copyright 2004
Website: www.7thunders.com

Cards of Your Destiny: What Your Birthday Reveals About You and Your Past, Present and Future by Robert Lee Camp
Copyright 1998 2004
Website: www.7thunders.com

Love and Destiny: Discover the Secret Language of Relationships by Sharon Jeffers
Copyright 2008
Website: www.starofthemagi.com

Face Value: Understanding the Evolution of Numbers in Playing Cards by Gina E. Jones
Copyright 2014
Website: www.thecardsoflife.com

Beverly Barrett Flintom has worked in the media for 27 years as a morning show co-host, television personality and voiceover artist. She has a Bachelors Degree in Broadcast Journalism with an emphasis in radio-tv from Eastern New Mexico University. She is single with one son named Denver and a dog named Charlie (A Joker always has a dog at their feet). She currently resides in Jacksonville, Florida.

Beverly is available for forecast readings and relationship readings. She can be contacted through her website yourcardisyourdestiny.com

FOUNDING MEMBER
International Association
of Cardology

Made in United States
Orlando, FL
01 August 2022

20456636R00024